pilates

Written by Michael Mann

FUBLISHING PLC

Published by Top That! Publishing plc
Tide Mill Way, Woodbridge, Suffolk, IP12 1AP, UK
www.topthatpublishing.com

0 2 4 6 8 9 7 5 3 1
Printed and bound in China

CW01597447

Contents

Introduction

Pilates is a method of exercise and physical movement designed to stretch, strengthen and balance the body.

Having attracted worldwide media attention, through being practised by celebrities, it was first devised by Joseph Pilates in the 1920s.

The exercises are based on learning to breathe correctly and, through controlled actions, improve flexibility, stability and posture.

Pilates brings many benefits, to mind and body, and is a great modern exercise because it is ideal for people with hectic lives. Most of the exercises in this book can be done at home, fitted into your day as you choose.
The book is broken up into sections that work different parts of the body. Within each section the moves become progressively harder but you should build up to the more difficult exercises slowly – no pose should cause discomfort.

To begin with, choose a variety of exercises from the different sections and create your own programme (which can be 15–60 minutes long, just go at your own pace).

How Pilates Works

Practised correctly, Pilates yields many benefits. Deep, breathing increases lung capacity and improves circulation. The exercising of the abdomen and back muscles directly benefits the body's core strength and flexibility. Muscular coordination is improved, as are posture and balance. Perhaps more surprisingly, bone density and joint health also benefit, and many people experience positive body awareness for the first time. Pilates teaches balance and control – a valuable lesson for both the mind and the body.

Breathing

Breathing is at the foundation of all the exercises because, if done correctly, it improves circulation. You should always breathe in through the nose and out through the mouth, making both the inward breath and the outward breath full. By getting your breathing right during the exercises your respiration throughout the rest of the day will improve.

Control

In Pilates, when the mind and the body are working as one you have achieved control. To do this, you need to concentrate on the movement, and think of nothing but the exercise. This will help you to obtain a near-perfect performance and the risk of injury will be minimal.

Centring the Body

Building strength around the core of the body is what is meant by centring in Pilates. Emphasis is placed on the abdominal muscles which are used to maintain support for the spine. Their power is used to start and control movements.

Stability

Stability is used to improve the posture and also the strength of a particular movement. The aim here is to be able to move one section of the body without moving another at the same time. Maintaining this stillness in the body as it moves is accomplished by using the abdominal muscles.

Flexibility

Pilates aims to improve the flexibility of the entire body. To achieve this, the body needs to go through its full range of movement without hyperextension, that is without going beyond the body's natural range.

Equipment

If you attend a Pilates studio you will find equipment there which supports the body or offers resistance. However, the exercises described in this book can be performed with items you will find around the home.

Clothing

It is important that you are comfortable at all times, so clothing matters. Do not wear anything that's so tight that it restricts the body's movement and equally, don't wear clothes that are so loose, that material can get in the way. Perform the exercises in bare feet or you can keep your socks on as they will help to prevent cramp.

Equipment

You should always take care to protect the back so it is important to have a towel or mat to lie on. In movements that require the legs to be still and the pelvis to be neutral, a pillow or a small cushion between the legs helps to maintain the correct position. A second towel roll or a small cushion can also be used to support the neck. This will help to keep the neck long and the body in the correct position.

Dumbbells

Dumbbells can be used to improve the upper body movements but they are not important. If you do decide to use them keep the weights down to 900g–1.4 kg (2–3 lb). For some of the leg exercises you may choose to use ankle weights. They should weigh no more than 450–900 g (1–2 lb). However, it is often better to work without weights.

Resistance Band

If you like, you can use a resistance band to increase the effort required for some exercises.

Medical Issues

Pilates is a safe and low-impact form of exercise but medical advice should be sought before embarking on a new programme, particularly by:

- Pregnant women;
- People aged forty years or more;
- People with a pre-existing medical condition such as heart disease;
- People with pre-existing musculoskeletal injuries or disorders;
- Anyone who has not exercised for a long time;
- Those who are very overweight.

Not all pilates movements are right for everybody, so if you find a position difficult or painful, don't continue with it.

Injuries

There is never any point in trying to exercise through pain, no matter how minor you may regard the injury. Only if your GP indicates that you can continue working on the rest of the body without further damaging the injured area should you carry on. When the injury has had sufficient time to heal you can use Pilates to take the rehabilitation a stage further and improve the strength and flexibility of the damaged area.

Back Pain

Do not perform Pilates exercises if you have a back problem, unless you know exactly what is wrong and have been advised that the exercises will be beneficial. Performing the wrong exercise is likely to cause further damage to the problematic area.

Medical Issues

Sprains

A sprain is when a ligament and/or surrounding tissues are damaged. It occurs when there has been a history of over-twisting of a joint. There will be swelling and possibly discolouration. To treat a sprain, keep your weight off the area until the initial pain has receded and place a cold compress around the affected area. Support the injured area with a bandage and avoid putting weight on it until it is completely healed. This may take up to two weeks.

Strains

A strain occurs when a muscle has been partially torn by over stretching. You will feel a sudden sharp pain, there may be some swelling and you may suffer from cramp. The treatment is the same as for a sprain.

Dislocation

A dislocation is when a bone has come out of its joint. This is a painful injury and should be treated in hospital. Never try to push the bone back into its joint as this can cause further damage to the blood vessels, nerves and surrounding tissue. If you have ever suffered from a dislocation then you should restrict your routine to a prescribed set of exercises given to you by your GP.

Diabetes

If you suffer from diabetes make sure you have some water handy and monitor your glucose level.

Pregnancy

Pilates can be performed during pregnancy but only if it has been part of your daily routine for some time and you have mastered the basic skills. You should refrain from working the abdominal muscles during the first and second trimesters and always work with a Pilates teacher on a one-to-one basis.

Asthma

Asthma causes recurrent episodes of breathlessness, wheezing and sometimes a dry cough. Episodes can be triggered by allergic reactions to certain products, dust and animal fur. Pilates cannot cure asthma but it can help to lessen the severity of an attack because of its emphasis on the use of the abdominal muscles when breathing.

Multiple Sclerosis

Multiple sclerosis, and other neuromuscular disorders, affect sufferers in different ways so Pilates will not be of benefit to everyone. However, some light body work can help to maintain body strength and flexibility. When working out, keep the movements simple and relaxed and stop as soon as you feel you have had enough.

Focus on the movements that encourage core stability rather than strength. Pelvic tilts, hip rolls and the gentler stomach movements are most likely to be beneficial.

About The Body

A well-balanced Pilates programme can tone and strengthen the entire body. To get the most from your routine it helps to learn more about the workings of your body.

Legs

For the purposes of Pilates, the leg muscles can be divided into three main groups: glutes (gluteus/glutei), hamstrings and quads (quadriceps).

The glutes are made up of the maximus, medius and minimus. Their functions are hip extension, external rotation, transverse abduction and adduction.

The hamstrings consist of the biceps femoris (long and short heads), the semitendinosus and the semimembranosus muscles. The functions of these muscles are to bend the knee, internal and external rotation and also hip extension.

The quads consist of the rectus femorus, vastus lateralis, intermedius and medials. Their functions are knee extension and rectus femerus hip flexion as well.
All of these muscles are balanced by further groups which support these functions.

Pelvic Floor

The pelvic floor is made up of a sheet of muscle that connects one side of the pelvis to the other. The muscle here is placed under a great deal of stress, particularly by women who give birth naturally, as the baby has to pass through the muscle itself.

The weight of the abdominal area also presents problems for the pelvic floor. Excessive weight here can lead to problems such as incontinence. By encouraging the abdominal muscles to take control over a movement, and encouraging the pelvic floor to be engaged in any movement, Pilates can alleviate this problem.

About The Body

Abdomen

In Pilates, the abdominal muscles are of vital importance. They are used to support the spine, to encourage the diaphragm to operate more efficiently and to encourage the pelvic floor to be more responsive. The abdominal muscles are made up of four sections: the transverse abdominal, the rectus abdominis and the internal and external obliques.

The transverse abdominal is a deep muscle that sits below the other abdominal muscles. It forms a girdle around the body's centre, supporting the spine and internal organs.

The rectus abdominal is used to flex the trunk and to draw the body forwards.

The internal and external obliques sit to the side and form the waist. They assist the body's rotation and side bends. Along with the transverse abdominal they also help with exhalation.

Back

The spine is made up of five sections, made up of 33 bones called vertebrae. Starting at the top of the spine, there are seven vertebrae that make up the cervical region. The first of these vertebrae supports the skull.

Next, there is the thoracic region. Each of these twelve vertebrae supports a pair of ribs. These structures are capable of very little motion because they are attached to the ribs. Following that is the lumbar region, where the five largest and strongest vertebrae are found. This area of the spine, as well as surrounding tissues, can cause 'low back pain'.

About The Body

The lumbar region has five vertebral bodies that are stacked on top of each other with a disc in between each one. The vertebral bodies act together to support about half the weight of the body, with the other half supported by muscles.

The vertebral bodies are attached to a bony arch, through which all the nerve roots run. Part of the arch comprises the paired facet joints which, in combination with the disc, create a three-joint complex at each vertebral motion segment.

The facet joints have cartilage on each surface and a capsule around them. The cartilage can degenerate with age. The three-joint complex at each vertebral segment allows for motion in flexion, extension, rotation and lateral bending.

Fifty per cent of flexion (bending forwards) occurs at the hips, and fifty per cent occurs at the lower (lumbar) spine. The motion is divided between the five motion segments in the lumbar spine, although a disproportionate amount of the motion falls on two of these segments. Consequently, these segments are the most likely to degenerate and cause pain with excess movement as they break down.

Lastly, there is the sacrum (five fused vertebrae) and the coccyx or tailbone (four fused vertebrae).

Head

The head is held on the spinal column, the topmost section of which is called the cervical portion. Each cervical vertebra is supported by a series of muscles that connect between the vertebrae and then from the ribcage and clavicle to the skull.

The head is crucial to all forms of movement. If the head drops it creates tension in the neck, shoulders and back. By keeping the chin tucked in during Pilates, the length of the neck is increased and muscles can be more effectively stretched.

About The Body

Shoulders

The shoulder girdle consists of a series of movements between the clavicle, the scapula and the humerus. The shoulder has the greatest range of movement in the whole of the body. The movements are passive by nature and occur as a result of active movement of the scapula. The clavicle acts as a stabilising strut to support the upper torso and to enable a greater range of movement.

The shoulder joint enables arm movement from the humerus and glenoid cavity. The highly mobile scapula is suspended over the ribcage by a series of muscles which increase the movement potential of the shoulder. Today, many people spend much of their time hunched over a computer or desk. The lowering of the head and rounding of the shoulders causes some strain to the neck, shoulders, the thoracic and lumbar spine. This condition should be addressed before embarking on a complete exercise routine.

Sit on a straight-backed chair and begin by opening the shoulders and then drawing them together. This will help to open the chest muscles and encourage you to sit up straight. Aim to feel the shoulders 'dropping' down the back as this will help to align the body. By stretching the shoulders and scapulae a little more each time you perform the movement, your neck and shoulders will soon feel relaxed.

Focus on your breathing when you perform the movement. As you breathe out, feel the navel drawing towards the spine and as you breathe in, feel the ribcage expand out to the sides. The effect is to encourage correct posture.

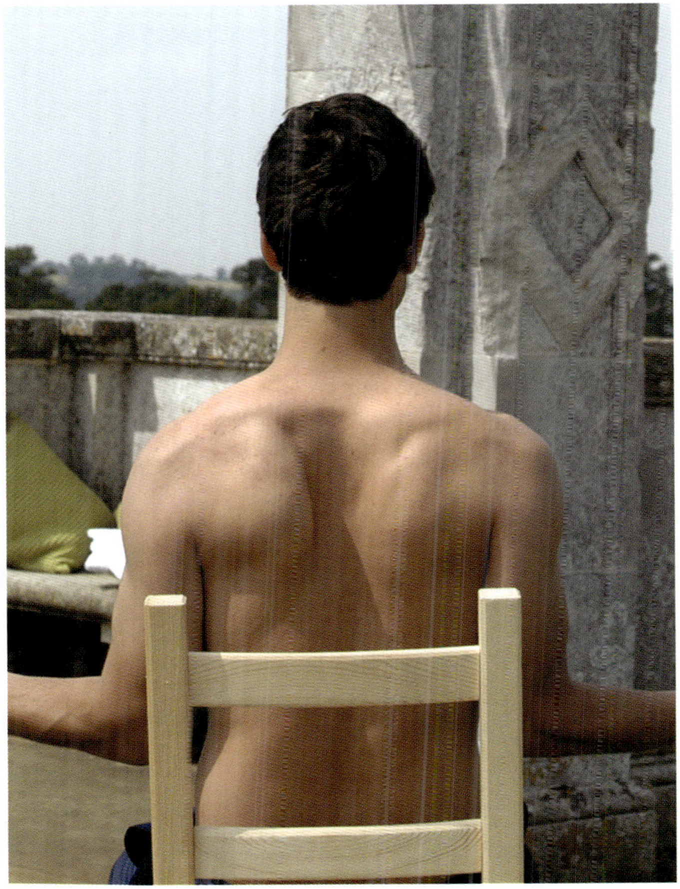

About The Body

Neutral Spine

Most people's lumbar section of the spine has a concave curve that points towards the centre of the body. A few people have essentially flat backs and even fewer have convex lumbar regions. When Pilates practitioners talk about keeping a neutral spine they mean maintaining a concave spine. The spine is not dropped towards the floor or lifted but maintains its natural position throughout the movement.

Posture

Bad posture is extremely common today. A quick solution is to sit on a straight-backed chair with your chin tucked in to keep the neck feeling long. Then imagine that you are being pulled up towards the sky by a piece of string going through the top of your head. Look forwards but don't look down or up. Gently drop your shoulders back and open the chest so that the breastbone is forward. As you breathe out, draw the navel towards the spine and, as you breathe in, feel the ribcage gently expand out to the sides. To further support the spine, the pelvis should be relaxed with the feet directly under the hips and the weight evenly distributed between the balls of the feet and the heels.

Feet

Maintaining the correct feet position will help to maintain the body's position throughout a movement. When standing or sitting you should be able to feel the balls of the feet and the heels.

The weight must be evenly distributed so you can feel a triangle across the sole of the foot. The foot has three types of movement: supernator, pronation and neutral.

A supernator movement is when a person walks on the outside of the foot, pronation is flat feet. Both can cause back problems.

The neutral position is when your walk covers the whole of the foot without the instep touching the floor. While this is the ideal it is hard to maintain.

Warm-Up Exercises

Exercise 1: Spider

As with any exercise programme, it's important to warm the body up. Perform all of these preparation exercises before beginning your routine.

Starting Position

Stand facing a wall with your feet hip width apart. You should be able to feel the balls and heels of your feet and the weight should be evenly distributed across the feet (A).

Keep your shoulders soft and tuck in your chin so that your neck feels long. Place your hands on the wall at shoulder height. While performing this warm-up exercise expand the ribcage out to the sides as you breathe in and as you breathe out draw the navel towards the spine.

Movement

1. Breathe in and out to prepare.

2. As you breathe in, gently walk your fingers up the wall – as if each hand is a spider – as high as you can (B).

3. As you breathe out, slide your hands back to the starting position.

4. Complete the exercise five times.

A.

B.

Warm-Up Exercises

Exercise 2: Arm Stretch

Starting Position

Stand with your feet hip width apart. You should be able to feel the balls of your feet and the heels. Put your hands by your sides.

Movement

1. Breathe in and place your left hand on your hip, stretching your right hand up to the sky.
2. As you breathe out, stretch your right arm over to the left of the body (A).
3. As you breathe in, take your right hand back so it points up again.
4. Complete the exercise five times and then change sides and repeat.

A.

Exercise 3: Back Curl

Starting Position

Stand with your feet hip width apart. Tuck in your chin so the neck feels long and relax your shoulder blades.

Movement

1. Breathe in to prepare.
2. As you breathe out, gently drop your arms towards the floor, feeling the back gently curl forwards (A).
3. Breathe in.
4. As you breathe out, gently curl the spine back up again, keeping the pelvis tilted forward. When you reach the top, raise your chin and look forwards.
5. Repeat five times.

A.

Warm-Up Exercises

Exercise 4: Lower Back Stretch

Starting Position

Lie on your back, bend your knees and place your feet hip width apart flat on the floor (A).

Movement

1. Breathe in to prepare.
2. As you breathe out, draw your knees halfway towards your chest, stretching your lower back out. Hold the knees with your hands and breathe in.
3. As you breathe out, bring your knees close to your chest (B).
4. As you breathe in, take your knees back until they are halfway between the ground and your chest.
5. Complete the exercise five times and then gently lower your legs.

A.

B.

Shoulder Mobility Exercises

When working at a desk or computer the tendency is for the shoulders to be pushed forwards and for the head to be tucked in towards the chest. The muscles of the back are taking all the strain and the shoulder blades draw out so far that the amount of movement the arms have is reduced. The movements included in this section are designed to alleviate this problem by opening the shoulders out. They have a further benefit in that once this has been achieved the quality of other exercises will be improved.

The specific aims of this section are:

1. To increase shoulder mobility and to release tension.

2. To exercise the waist and abdominal muscles.

The muscles used include the trapezius, the major and minor rhomboids, serratus antera, latimus dorsi and supraspinatus.

Shoulder Mobility Exercises

Exercise 1: Palms Ups

Starting Position

Sit on a straight-backed dining room chair with your feet flat on the floor. You should be able to feel the heels and the balls of your feet. Your back should be straight and the chin should be tucked in to make your neck feel long. Tuck in your elbows and place your forearms at right angles to the body. Your palms should be facing up (A).

Movement

1. Breathe in and, as you do so, take your hands out to the side, keeping the elbows tucked in (B).

2. As you breathe out, return to the starting position, drawing the navel towards the spine, as you do so.

3. Complete the exercise five times and then repeat, another five times with your palms facing downwards.

A.

B.

Shoulder Mobility Exercises

Exercise 2: Palms Up and Stretch Out to the Side

Starting Position

Assume the same starting position as for Exercise 1 on page 18.

Movement

1. Breathe in and, as you do so, take your hands round to the side, keeping the elbows tucked in.
2. As you breathe out, push your arms out to the side so that your forearms raise a little. Drop your shoulders (A).
3. Breathe in and bring the elbows back to the waist.
4. Breathe out and bring the arms back to the front of the body.
5. Complete the exercise five times.

A.

Shoulder Mobility Exercises

Exercise 3: Shoulder Shrug

Starting Position

Assume the same starting position as for Exercise 1, except that this time you should keep your hands by your sides (A).

Movement

1. Breathe in and, as you do so, draw up your shoulders as near as you can to your ears (B).

A.

2. As you breathe out, drop the shoulders back and down towards the waist.

3. Complete the exercise five times, keeping the shoulders back throughout the movement.

B.

Shoulder Mobility Exercises

Exercise 4: Circle

Starting Position

Assume the same starting position as for Exercise 1, but this time place your hands on your shoulders with your elbows out to the sides (A).

Movement

1. Breathe in and, as you do so, draw the shoulders forwards and up (B).
2. As you breathe out, drop the shoulders back and down behind the body. You will find that you are drawing a circle with your elbows.
3. Complete the exercise five times, then repeat it, drawing circles backwards and down; again for five repetitions.

Remember: As you breathe in expand the chest out and, on the outward breath draw the navel towards the spine. This act encourages the diaphragm to force air from the lungs and the transverse abdominal to take control of any movement in the mid-section of the back.

A.

B.

Exercise 5: Arm Extension

Starting Position

Assume the same starting position as for Exercise 1, but rest your hands gently in your lap.

Movement

1. Breathe in to prepare.

2. As you breathe out, extend your left arm. Take it behind your ear, gently extending the index finger (A).

3. As you breathe in, bring the arm back to just in front of the ear (B). Repeat this movement three times. Take the arm back a fourth time, but this time extend the stretch right back (C).

4. As you breathe in, sweep the hand round to the front of the body and stretch the arm up. Repeat the whole sequence three times, then repeat on the other side.

A.

B.

C.

Exercise 6: Side Stretch on a Chair

Starting Position

Sit sideways on a dining-room chair with your back straight. Tuck in your chin in order to lengthen the neck and stretch out your spine. Allow your shoulder blades to drop down your back towards the waist. Place your feet flat on the floor with the weight evenly distributed across both feet. Stretch your right hand across the body and place it on the back of the chair and stretch your left arm towards the sky.

Movement

1. Breathe in to prepare.
2. As you breathe out, take your left arm over to the right side of your head (A).
3. As you breathe in, bring it back to the starting position.
4. Complete the exercise five times, then swap arms and repeat with the right arm five times.

Remember: Keep the upward arm soft and lift from the shoulder throughout the movement, feeling your shoulder blades rise towards the sky.

A.

Shoulder Mobility Exercises

Exercise 7: Hand Drop

Starting Position

Sit normally on a dining-room chair, placing your arms by your sides. Your palms should be facing back (A).

Movement

1. Breathe in to prepare.
2. As you breathe out, gently drop your hands down towards the floor. Let your shoulder blades drop and push the palms back a little (B).
3. Breathe in and return to the starting position and repeat five times.

A.

B.

Spinal Mobility Exercises

All the movements within this section help to relax the muscles that support the spine and encourage the abdominal muscles to engage with the back.

The specific aims of this section are:

1. To relax and mobilise the lower back and the back as a whole.
2. To encourage abdominal control over the movements without exerting any tension on the rest of the body.
3. To relax and mobilise the pelvis, lumbar region and thorax.
4. To lengthen the spine and encourage abdominal support.
5. To strengthen the abdominal and oblique muscles.
6. To strengthen the lower back, hamstrings and glutes.

The first few exercises focus on the pelvis and coccyx (also called the tail bone) while the other exercises focus on the lumbar and the thoracic region. The five concave vertebral sections within the lumbar region have to cope with more movement than any other area of the back and require the support of the abdominal muscles. The thoracic region is the longest part of the spine and has twelve convex vertebrae. There is very little movement in this region as it is restricted by the ribcage.

Back Stability

The spine is made up of vertebral sections placed on top of one another. Each one requires a range of muscles to support them. These muscle groups work to allow the spine to move by extension, bending and rotation. They also act as links between the adjacent spinous processes of the vertebrae and are the deep spinal muscle.

The pelvis is a basin-shaped structure that supports the spinal column and protects the abdominal organs. The coccyx is formed by the fusion of four originally separated coccyges.

The pelvic floor, or pelvic diaphragm, is a sheet of muscles running from the front of the pelvis to the rear surface of the symphysis pubis to the ischia and coccyx. The pelvic floor supports the lower internal organs of the body. It can be damaged by childbirth, obesity problems and if the central nervous system has been compromised. During the pelvic exercises the abdominal muscle encourages the pelvic floor to engage, therefore helping to improve stability.

Spinal Mobility Exercises

Exercise 1: The Cat

Starting Position

Kneel, placing your hands flat on the floor directly under your shoulder blades. Your knees should be hip width apart, your toes pointing away from the body. The back should be straight and the chin tucked in, hold this position and breathe in.

Movement

1. Breathe out and, as you do so, roll the spine, from the pelvis to the neck, up towards the sky, curling the back vertebra by vertebra until the shoulders are at full stretch. Breathe in and hold the position (A).

A.

2. As you breathe out, gently tilt the pelvis and roll the back down in the opposite direction. Lift the head and look forwards (B).

3. Hold the position and breathe in. Complete the sequence five times.

B.

Spinal Mobility Exercises

Exercise 2: Pelvic Floor Tilt

A.

Starting Position

Lie on the floor on your back. Bend your knees and place your feet on the floor hip width apart. Relax your shoulders and draw the shoulder blades towards your waist, pulling them slightly into the centre of the body. Tuck your chin in so that your neck feels long. Place the lumbar in a neutral position and make sure your hips are comfortable on the floor. The weight should be evenly distributed across the buttocks (A).

Movement

B.

1. Breathe in to prepare.
2. Breathe out and draw the pelvic and abdominal muscles in towards the centre of the body (B).
3. Return to the starting position.
4. Complete the exercise five times.

Spinal Mobility Exercises

Exercise 3: Pelvic Tilt

Starting Position

Assume the same starting position as for Exercise 2 on page 27.

Movement

1. Breathe in to prepare.
2. As you breathe out, gently tilt the pelvis up, taking the buttocks off the floor. Breathe in and hold the pose.
3. As you breathe out, curl the pelvis back to the floor and into the neutral position ready to perform the next repetition (A).
4. Complete the exercise five times.

Remember: Do not rush the movement and keep the exercise soft and relaxed.

A.

Spinal Mobility Exercises

Exercise 4: Pelvic Tilt Half Lift

Starting Position

Assume the same starting position as for Exercise 2.

Movement

1. Breathe in to prepare.
2. As you breathe out, gently tilt the pelvis and roll the lumbar and thoracic spine off the floor, keeping the pelvis in a neutral position (A).
3. Hold this position as you breathe in.
4. Breathe out and return the spine and pelvis to the neutral position ready for the next lift.
5. Complete the exercise five times.

A.

Exercise 5: Pelvic Tilt Full Lift

Starting Position

Assume the same starting position as for Exercise 2.

Movement

1. Breathe in to prepare.
2. As you breathe out, gently tilt the pelvis up and roll the lumbar and the ribcage off the floor, vertebra by vertebra, as far as your shoulders (A).
3. Hold the position and then breathe in.
4. Breathe out as you roll the back down and gently tilt the pelvis back to the floor.
5. Complete the exercise five times. On the last repetition put the spine into a neutral position in preparation for the next pelvic exercise.

A.

Spinal Mobility Exercises

Exercise 6: Pelvic Tilt with Full Arm Extension

Starting Position

Assume the same starting position as in Exercise 2.

Movement

1. Breathe in to prepare.
2. As you breathe out, tilt the pelvis and roll the lumbar and ribcage off the floor vertebra by vertebra as far as the shoulders, as high as you can.
3. As you breathe in, stretch the shoulder blades and lift the arms up and, if you can, take them back overhead so that they rest on the ground behind (A).
4. As you breathe out, roll the spine back vertebra by vertebra, and then tilt the pelvis back to the floor.
5. Breathe in and return the arms back to your sides, stretching them out as you do so.
6. Complete the exercise five times.

Remember: If you are unable to rest your arms on the floor comfortably, stretch them towards the sky instead.

A.

Exercise 7: Hip Roll, Legs Together

Starting Position

Lie on the floor on your back with your knees bent and squeezed together, feet on the floor. Relax your shoulders, drawing the shoulder blades towards your waist. Tuck in your chin so that the neck feels long. The lumbar should be in a neutral position, the hips relaxed and comfortable on the floor with the weight evenly distributed across the buttocks (A).

Movement

1. Breathe in to prepare.

2. Breathe out. Keeping the knees together, take them over to one side without allowing the spine to leave the floor (B).

3. Hold the position for a breath and return to the starting position.

4. Complete the exercise five times then repeat on the other side.

A.

B.

Exercise 8: Hip Roll, Legs Apart

Starting Position

Assume the same position as in Exercise 2.

Movement

1. Breathe in to prepare.
2. As you breathe out, take the knees over to the side just a little (keeping them apart). Do not allow the spine to leave the floor.
3. Hold the position for a breath and then return to the starting position.
4. Complete the exercise five times and then repeat on the other side.

A.

Exercise 9: Hip Roll with Leg Extension

Starting Position

Assume the same starting position as for Exercise 2 (A).

Movement

1. Breathe in to prepare.
2. As you breathe out, take the knees over to the left just a little, without allowing the spine to leave the floor.
3. Stretch the right leg out and hold the position (B).
4. Breathe in and return the leg to the floor and bring the knees into the starting position.
5. Complete the exercise five times and then repeat with the other leg.

A.

B.

Spinal Mobility Exercises

Exercise 10: Hip Roll with Legs in a Tabletop Extension 1

Starting Position

Lie on your back with your knees bent and your feet flat on the floor. Stretch your arms out to the side at shoulder level. Lift your legs up so that your knees are at a right angle to your hips and you form a tabletop position (A).

Movement

1. Breathe in to prepare.

2. As you breathe out, take the knees about 20 cm over to one side, keeping them at right angles to your hips. Make sure the spine doesn't leave the floor (B)

3. Hold the position for a breath and then return to the starting position.

4. Complete the exercise five times, then repeat the sequence, taking the legs to the other side.

A.

B.

Exercise 11: Hip Roll with Legs in a Tabletop Extension 2

A.

B.

Starting Position

Assume the tabletop starting position as for Exercise 10 (A).

Movement

1. Breathe in to prepare.
2. As you breathe out, take the legs over to one side a little and fully extend them (B).
3. Hold the position for a breath and then bring the legs back into the tabletop position.
4. As you breathe out, take the legs over to the other side and repeat.
5. Complete the exercise ten times, alternating the sides.

Remember: Keep the spine neutral throughout the movement.

Spinal Mobility Exercises

Exercise 12: Knee Lift

Starting Position

Lie on the floor on your back with your feet on the floor. Bend your knees, squeezing them together. Relax your shoulders, drawing the shoulder blades down towards your waist. Tuck your chin in so that the neck feels long. The lumbar should be in a neutral position, the hips relaxed and comfortable on the floor with the weight evenly distributed across the buttocks (A).

Movement

1. Breathe in to prepare.
2. As you breathe out, lift the left foot a little off the floor. Don't push the foot up but lift it with the thigh muscles (B).
3. Hold the position breathe in and then return to the starting position.
4. Repeat the movement, this time using your right leg. Complete the exercise ten times, alternating legs.

A.

B.

Exercise 13: Knee Lift with a Turn Out

A.

B.

Starting Position

Assume the same starting position as for Exercise 12.

Movement

1. Breathe in to prepare.
2. As you breathe out, lift the left foot off the floor (A) so that the knee is over the hip. Without moving the pelvis, turn the leg out to the side (B).
3. Hold the position, breath in and then draw the knee back to the centre and return the foot to the floor, maintaining a neutral spine as you do so.
4. Repeat the movement, this time using the right leg.
5. Complete the exercise ten times, performing five repetitions with each leg.

Remember: Keep the buttocks in contact with the floor throughout the movement. Don't tilt the pelvis and keep the spine neutral.

Spinal Mobility Exercises

Exercise 14: Leg Extension in Tabletop Position

Starting Position

Lie on the floor on your back with your knees bent in a tabletop position. Relax your shoulders and draw your shoulder blades towards your waist, pulling them slightly into the centre so that the chest is opened. Tuck your chin in so that your neck feels long. Your arms should be by your sides (A).

Movement

1. Breathe in and as you exhale lift your legs up so that they are at a right angle to your body. Your knees should be in line with your hips. Breathe in.
2. Breathe out and, as you do so, stretch your left leg a little (B).
3. Hold the position for a breath in and then return to the starting position.
4. Repeat the movement, this time using the right leg.
5. Complete the exercise ten times, alternating the legs.

A.

B.

Abdominal Exercises

This section works on the abdominal part of the body. The aim is to create the core stability and strength that the body needs throughout the day and to help prevent injury to the spine. The four main muscles used in this section are: the transverse abdominal, rectus abdominis and the internal and external obliques. The psoai are used for some of the more strenuous exercises.

The first exercises are done with a neutral spine. This means that the spine should be kept in a comfortable position and not forced either up or down.

This section also encourages the rectus abdominis to work a little harder. Make sure you end your abdominal work with a stretch and then a movement into the rest position to relax the back and relieve any tension that might have built up.

Do not carry on if your back or neck is causing any discomfort. If you are having trouble lifting your head try using a rolled up towel at the base of the skull, holding on to either side with the elbows back.

Abdominal Exercises

Exercise 1: Head Raiser

Starting Position

Lie flat on the floor on your back. Bend your knees and place your feet hip width apart flat on the floor. Place your hands behind your head, at the base of the skull (A). Relax the shoulders and draw the shoulder blades down towards your waist, pulling them slightly into the centre. Tuck the chin in so that the neck feels long and stretched. The lumbar should be in a neutral position, the hips relaxed and the weight evenly distributed across the buttocks.

A.

Movement

1. Breathe in to prepare.

2. As you breathe out, slowly raise your head and shoulders a little (B).

3. Breathe in and return to the starting position slowly, trying to keep the spine neutral.

4. Complete the exercise five times.

B.

Abdominal Exercises

Exercise 2: Head Raiser with Knee Lift

Starting Position

Assume the same starting position as for Exercise 1 on page 41.

Movement

1. Breathe in to prepare.
2. As you breathe out, lift your head and upper body off the floor. At the same time, use your abdominal muscles to lift your right leg off the floor (A).
3. As you breathe in, return the head and foot to the floor.
4. Repeat the movement, this time using your left leg.
5 Complete the exercise ten times, alternating the legs.

A.

Exercise 3: Head Raiser with Knee Lift and Turn

Starting Position

Assume the same starting position as for Exercise 1 on page 41.

Movement

1. Breathe in to prepare.
2. As you breathe out, raise the head and upper body off the floor. At the same time, use your abdominal muscles to lift your left leg off the floor. At the highest point of the movement, turn your head so that your left knee is in your direct line of vision (B).
3. Return the head to the centre and then lower your upper body and leg to the floor.
4. Complete ten repetitions, alternating which knee you are lifting and which way you are pointing your head.

A.

Abdominal Exercises

Exercise 4: 100s

Starting Position

Lie on the floor on your back with your knees bent and your feet off the floor in a tabletop position. Relax your shoulders and draw the shoulder blades towards the waist, pulling them in slightly so that the chest is opened. Tuck your chin in so the neck feels long. Your arms should be by your sides, palms down (A).

Movement

1. Breathe in to prepare.

2. As you breathe out, cross your ankles and lift your head and arms off the floor (B).

3. Hold the position breathing in then breathing out, each for a count of five. Draw the navel in with the outward breath.

4. When you have completed a breath return the head and legs to the floor.

A.

B.

Exercise 5: Single Leg Stretch

Starting Position

Assume the same starting position as for Exercise 4 on page 44.

Movement

1. Breathe in to prepare.

2. As you breathe out, take a light hold of the inside of your left knee with your right hand (A). Your left hand should be holding your left ankle. Stretch the right leg away from the body, pointing the toes. Draw the navel into the spine as you do so (B).

3. As you breathe in, draw the extended leg back to the centre again.

4. Reverse the arms so that the left hand is on the right knee and the right hand is on the right ankle and extending the left leg (C). Complete ten repetitions, alternating the legs.

A.

B.

C.

Abdominal Exercises

Exercise 6: Single Leg Lowering

Starting position

Lie on the floor with your legs in the tabletop position. Stretch your arms up towards the sky (A).

Movement

1. Breathe in to prepare.

2. As you breathe out, raise your head and upper body. Stretch the legs away so that the body is in a 'V' shape and lower your arms to the ground or just above (B).

3. As you breathe in, lower the right leg a little towards the ground (C).

4. Breathe out and lift the lower leg in line with the other leg and return to the starting position. Repeat ten times, alternating legs.

A.

B.

C.

Exercise 7: Roll Down

Starting Position

Sit on the floor with your legs stretched out in front of the body and flex your feet. Raise your arms level with your shoulders, but keep them relaxed and draw your shoulder blades down towards your waist. Tuck your chin in so that the neck feels long (A).

Movement

1. Breathe in to prepare.

2. As you breathe out, gently roll the spine down onto the floor. Then stretch your arms behind the head to the ground (B).

3. As you breathe in, draw your arms back over the head and gently return the back to the starting position. Stretch forwards then return to the centre to complete the sequence again.

4. Complete the exercise five times.

A.

B.

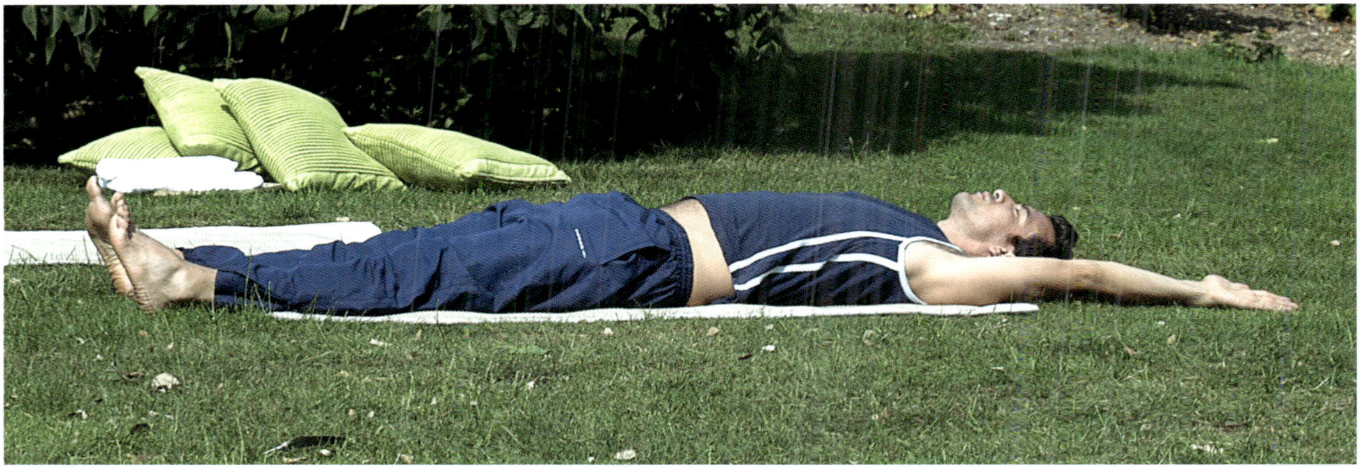

Exercise 8: Scissors

Starting Position

Lie on your back with your legs in the tabletop position, arms raised towards the sky. Tuck your chin in (A).

Movement

1. Breathe in to prepare.

2. As you breathe out, curl the body upwards into a 'V', stretching the legs out and lowering the arms to the side. Hold this position (B).

3. As you breathe in, part the legs so that they are a little more than hip width apart. Flex the feet (C).

4. As you breathe out, draw the legs together and cross your ankles (D). Point the toes (E), then repeat steps 3 and 4 five times

A.

B.

C.

D.

E.

Exercise 9: Cobra

Starting Position

Lie on the floor on your front with your arms stretched out, palms down. Your legs should also be stretched out, with the toes pointed. Your chin should be tucked in so that the neck feels long (A).

Movement

1. Breathe in to prepare.
2. Draw your hands towards your body, so that the arms form a right angle with the elbows.
3. As you breathe out, gently stretch the lower back and the abdominal muscles and hold for five slow breaths.
4. Walk the arms back and return to the starting position.

A.

B.

Abdominal Exercises

Exercise 10: Rest Position

Starting Position

Assume the same starting position as for Exercise 9 on page 49.

Movement

1. Breathe in to prepare.
2. Draw your arms up so that your hands are under your shoulders (A).
3. As you breathe out, gently lift yourself on to your hands and knees (B).
4. Gently sit back on your heels and allow your arms to stretch out in front of you (C).
5. Rest your forehead on the floor. Hold the stretch, breathing in and out as you do so.
6. Return to the starting position.

A.

B.

C.

Leg and Thigh Exercises

It is not just the muscles within the legs and thighs that affect the movement of the lower body; the abdominal muscles are also influential. The transverse abdominal and the psoai help to control and support any action undertaken by the quadriceps, gluteus, adductor, hamstrings and calf muscles.

During the next set of movements it is these muscles that are going to be worked on. The exercises will help to give strength and flexibility to the legs, the powerhouse from which the body gets its forward motion.

Although the first three exercises seem very similar, each one works on a different muscle group, while still encouraging the core muscle to maintain support for the body.

Leg and Thigh Exercises

Exercise 1: Straight Leg Lift Parallel

Starting Position

Lie on the floor on your back. Bend your knees and place your feet hip width apart on the floor. Relax your shoulders and draw the shoulder blades down towards your waist, pulling them slightly into the centre. Tuck your chin in so the neck feels long. The lumbar should be in a neutral position, the hips relaxed and the weight evenly distributed across the buttocks (A).

A.

B.

Movement

1. Breathe in and, as you do so, stretch the right leg out along the floor and then point the toes (B).

2. As you breathe out, raise the right leg up until it is level with the left knee. Flex the foot and hold the pose (C).

3. Breathe in as you gently lower the leg.

4. Complete five repetitions and then repeat the movement with the other leg.

C.

Leg and Thigh Exercises

Exercise 2: Straight Leg Lift and Turn Out

Starting Position

Assume the same starting position as for Exercise 1 on page 52.

Movement

1. Breathe in and, as you do so, stretch out the right leg along the floor, turn it from the hip and point the foot.
2. As you breathe out, lift the right leg up until it is parallel with the left knee. Flex the foot (A).
3. Breathe in as you gently lower the leg to the floor, keeping your foot flexed.
4. Complete the exercise five times and then repeat the movement, reversing the legs.

Remember: When lifting the legs use the abdominal muscles and keep the back neutral.

A.

Exercise 3: Top Leg Lift

Starting Position

Lie on the floor on one side. Extend the lower arm out along the floor with your palm down. Bend your lower leg and extend the top leg. Place the top hand on your hip with the elbow high. Drop the top shoulder blade down the back and towards the waist. Keep the back relaxed and the neck long (A).

Movement

1. Breathe in to prepare.
2. Breathe out and, using the abdominal muscles, lift the top leg up no higher than your hip. Keep the foot flexed throughout the movement and use your hand to maintain the position of the hip (B).
3. Breathe in and return to the starting position.
4. Complete the exercise five times and then turn over and repeat on the other side.

A.

B.

Exercise 4: Top Leg Forward and Lift

Starting Position

Assume the same starting position as for Exercise 3 on page 54.

Movement

1. Breathe in to prepare and flex the top foot.

2. As you breathe out, stretch the top leg out and lift it to hip height.

3. Breathe in and bring the leg forwards so that it is at a right angle to the body.

4. As you breathe out, lift the leg a little higher (A).

5. As you breathe in, lower the leg.

6. Complete the five lifts then as you breathe out, return the leg to the starting position. Repeat the sequence with the other leg.

A.

Leg and Thigh Exercises

Exercise 5: Bottom Leg Lift

Starting Position

Lie on the floor on your side. Bend your top leg forwards and rest it on the ground. Stretch the bottom leg out, flexing the lower foot. Place your top hand on your hip. Keep the elbow pointed towards the sky. The right arm should be stretched out along the floor with the palm facing downwards. Keep the top arm relaxed throughout the exercise (A).

Movement

1. Breathe in to prepare.
2. As you breathe out, stretch the lower leg away from the body and lift it off the floor. Keep the foot flexed throughout (B).
3. As you breathe in, return to the starting position.
4. Complete the exercise five times and then turn over and repeat on the other side.

A.

B.

Exercise 6: Double Leg Lift

Starting Position

Lie on the floor on your side. Extend the bottom arm out along the floor with your palm down. Stretch your legs out along the floor and point your toes. Place the other hand on the floor with the elbow high and drop the shoulder blade down the back and towards the waist. Keep the back relaxed and tuck the chin in to make the neck feel long (A).

Movement

1. Breathe in to prepare.

2. As you breathe out stretch both legs away from the body, lifting them a little way off the ground (B).

3. Breathe in and, as you do so, return the legs to the starting position.

4. Complete the exercise five times and then repeat on the other side.

Remember: Use the abdominal muscles to support the back throughout this movement.

A.

B.

Spinal Strengthening Exercises

The movements within this section are intended to help with the lower back. The muscle located under the erector group, is often missed. However, in relation to lower back pain, it is one of the most important muscles. It is the only muscle with fibres attached to the posterior part of the sacrum and provides stability for the spine.

Spinal muscles and ligaments attach to the vertebrae, ribs, and pelvis to permit and manage various trunkal motions including – forward and backward bending, side to side bending, and rotation. When a spinal motion occurs in excess or a muscle is overworked injury occurs.

The soft tissues around the spine also play a key role in low back pain. The large paired muscles in the low back (erector spinae) help hold up the spine. With inflammation the muscles can spasm and cause pain. The aim of this section is to create stability by helping to build lower body strength without placing the spine under any major stress. The abdominal muscles will be encouraged to support the spine while also engaging the muscles of the spine. Keep all the movements small and draw the navel towards the spine for support.

Spinal Strengthening Exercises

Exercise 1: Leg Extension

Starting Position

Lie on the floor on your front with your forehead resting on your hands. Your shoulders should be soft and the neck long (A).

Movement

1. Breathe in to prepare.
2. As you breathe out, stretch the left leg away from the centre and up a little (B).
3. As you breathe in, lower the leg.
4. Repeat the exercise on the opposite leg, alternating the leg lifts until you have lifted each one five times.

A.

B.

Spinal Strengthening Exercises

Exercise 2: Knee Bend and Push

Starting Position

Assume the same starting position as for Exercise 1.

Movement

1. Breathe in and, as you do so, bend the left leg up at the knee and flex the foot.
2. As you breathe out, push the heel towards the sky a little, taking the thigh off the floor (A).
3. As you breathe in, lower the leg.
4. Complete five repetitions with each leg.

A.

Spinal Strengthening Exercises

Exercise 3: Back Extension

Starting Position

Lie on the floor on your front with your forehead resting on your hands. Relax your shoulders and draw your shoulder blades down towards your waist. Tuck your chin in to make your neck feel long and stretch your legs out along the floor. The lumbar should be in a neutral position (A).

Movement

1. Breathe in to prepare.
2. As you breathe out, gently raise your hands and upper body up (B).
3. Breathe in as you return to the starting position
4. Complete the exercise five times.

A.

B.

Exercise 4: Back Extension with Hands Drawn in

Starting Position

Lie on the floor on your front, with your forehead resting on the ground, your hands should be placed palms up by your sides (A).

A.

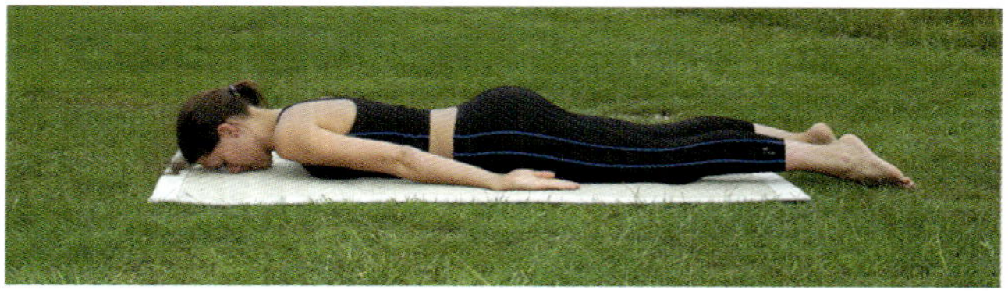

Movement

1. Breathe in to prepare.

2. As you breathe out, lift your arms and upper torso off the floor a little and stretch the arms up along your sides (B).

3. As you breathe in, return to the starting position.

4. Complete the exercise five times.

B.

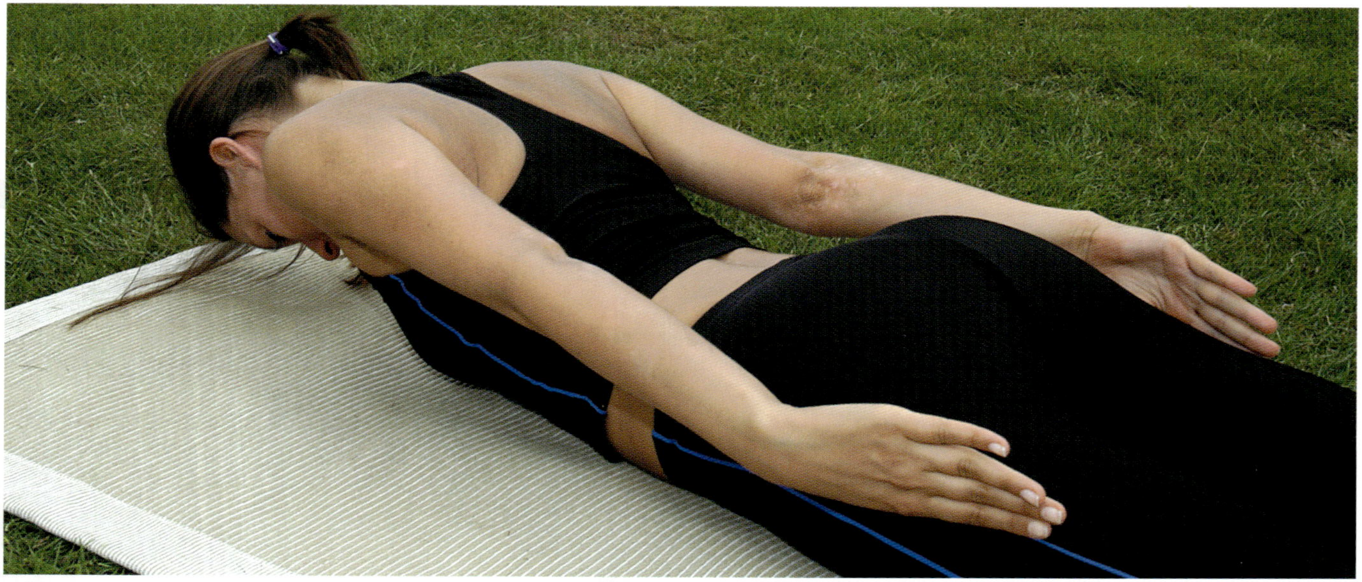

Spinal Strengthening Exercises

Exercise 5: Crawl

Starting Position

Lie on the floor on your front with your arms stretched out – palms down – in front of you. Tuck your chin in so that your neck feels long (A).

A.

Movement

1. Breathe in to prepare

2. As you breathe out, stretch your right arm and your left leg away from the body, lifting them a little off the floor (B).

3. As you breathe in, lower the arm and leg to the floor.

4. Breathe out and repeat on the opposite arm and leg.

5. Complete ten repetitions, alternating the leg and arm positions.

B.

Spinal Strengthening Exercises

Exercise 8: Spinal Stretch, Arms to the Sides

Starting Position

Lie on the floor on your front, resting your forehead on your hands (A).

Movement

1. Breathe in to prepare.
2. As you breathe out, lift your head, shoulders and upper body off the floor.
3. Breathe in and stretch your arms out to the sides (B).
4. As you breathe out, bend your arms back in, keeping your upper body off the floor.
5. Breathe in and lower your torso to the floor. Repeat the exercise five times.

A.

B.

Upper Body Exercises

The upper body exercises work the pectoralis (major and minor), trap and lats, which are the trapezius and latissimus dorsi muscles.

The pectoralis major and minor are the axial muscles responsible for flexing, adducting and rotating the arm medially. They originate on the clavicle, sternum, and cartilages of the second to sixth ribs and insert on the greater tubercle and interbubercular sulcus of the humerus.

The latissimus dorsi is one of two muscles which cross the shoulder joint. Its role is to extend and adduct the arm and rotate in the medial plane. Movement of the arm in the medial plane is either straight out in front of you or directly behind you.

The function of the trapezius is to elevate, retract and rotate the scapula; superior fibres elevate, middle fibres retract, and inferior fibres depress the scapula.

The exercises in this section are really basic shoulder work. They will help you to develop an open chest, allowing a free range of movement within the body and upper torso. You can perform these movements with a set of light weights if you wish.

Upper Body Exercises

Exercise 1: Wall Press Up, Single Arm

Starting Position

Stand in front of a wall with your feet hip width apart. Your shoulders should be relaxed and your chin tucked in to make the neck feel long. Place one hand on the wall at shoulder height, with your fingers pointing towards the sky, the elbow bent (A).

Movement

1. Breathe in to prepare.
2. Keeping the shoulder blades still, draw the breastbone towards the wall. Allow the nose to touch the wall (B).
3. Breathe out and gently push away, using your pectoral muscles. Draw the navel towards the spine to support the back.
4. Do the exercise five times then repeat on the other arm.

A.

B.

Exercise 2: Wall Press Up, Both Arms

Starting Position

Assume the same starting position as for Exercise 1, on page 66, but place both hands against the wall (A).

Movement

1. Breathe in and, as you do so, draw the body towards the wall, keeping your elbows out to the side. Allow your nose to touch the wall.

2. As you breathe out, push away from the wall.

3. Complete the exercise five times.

A.

B.

Exercise 3: Open Fly Standing

B.

Starting Position

A.

Stand with your feet hip width apart. Relax the shoulders and tuck the chin in to make the neck feel long. Take your arms out in front of the body, keeping the elbows and hands soft, pointing inwards (A).

Movement

1. Breathe in as you open the arms out to the side, drawing the shoulder blades together (B).

2. Bring the arms back together as you breathe out, pulling the navel in to the spine.

3. Complete the exercise five times.

Exercise 4: Circle Forwards

Starting Position

Assume the same starting position as for Exercise 3 on page 68.

Movement

1. Breathe in to prepare. Bring the arms up in front of the body and lift them towards the sky, keeping the elbows soft (A).

A.

2. Breathe out as you stretch the arms out to the side (B), bringing them down towards your thighs.

3. Breathe in as you gently draw the arms back in front of the body to the starting position.

4. Complete the exercise five times.

B.

Exercise 5: Circle Backwards

Starting Position

Stand with your feet hip width apart. Relax the shoulders and tuck the chin in. Hands hanging loosely at your sides.

Movement

1. Breathe in and, as you do so, gently bring the arms down in front of your body.
2. As you breathe out, stretch your arms up (A) from the front of your body, to the sky (B).
3. Breathe in as you return to the starting position (C).
4. Complete the exercise five times.

A.

B.

C.

Exercise 6: Alternating Stretch

Starting Position

Assume the same starting position as for Exercise 3 on page 68.

Movement

1. Breathe in to prepare.
2. As you breathe out, gently stretch your left hand in front of the body and up towards the sky. At the same time drop your right arm down to your thigh (A).
3. Breathe in as you return to the starting position.
4. Repeat the exercise, this time reversing the arms.
5. Complete the exercise five times for each arm.

A.

Exercise 7: Pectoral Stretch 1

Starting Position

Stand with your feet hip width apart. Place your hands on your buttocks. Tuck your chin in so the neck feels long.

Movement

1. Breathe in to prepare.
2. As you breathe out, draw the shoulder blades together and stretch out the chest. Hold the position for five breaths (A).
3. Complete the exercise five times.

A.

Exercise 8: Pectoral Stretch 2

Starting Position

Stand by a wall with your feet hip width apart and your right forearm on the wall. Draw the shoulder blades together and open the chest out (A).

A.

B.

Movement

1. Breathe in to prepare.

2. As you breathe out, gently move forwards, keeping the forearm on the wall. Hold the position for five breaths (B).

3. Relax and then repeat the exercise using your left arm.

Shoulder Mobility – Relaxation Exercises

Four joints support the shoulder and a complex series of muscles that allow a full range of movement. Among the main muscles the trapezius elevates, rotates and retracts the scapula, while the latissimus dorsi rotates the scapula down and adducts and medially rotates the humerus.

The pectoral muscles assist in stabilising the clavicle, adducting and medially rotating the humerus and flexing the arm. There are many other muscles involved here, including the deep muscles which help to support the shoulders and upper body and give stability to the neck.

In some occupations the shoulders and back come under a great deal of stress during the day. If you find it difficult to find enough time to perform a long routine, this session is an ideal way to relax the shoulders.

The routine forces the shoulders to stretch a little more each time.

Shoulder Mobility – Relaxation Exercises

Exercise 1: Shoulder Mobility 1

Starting Position

Lie on the floor on your side, placing a small pillow under your head. Bend both knees and extend your lower arm out in front of the body, palm facing up. Place the opposite hand on top of this one. Keep your shoulders back and your hip pointing towards the sky. Tuck the chin in to make the neck feel long (A).

Movement

1. Breathe in to prepare.
2. As you breathe out, keeping the hips and back still, slide the top hand along the lower hand, away from the body.
3. Breathe in and return the hand to the starting position.
4. Complete this exercise five times but do not turn over until you have completed Exercises 2, 3 and 4 on the following pages.

Remember: Do not rush the movement.

A.

B.

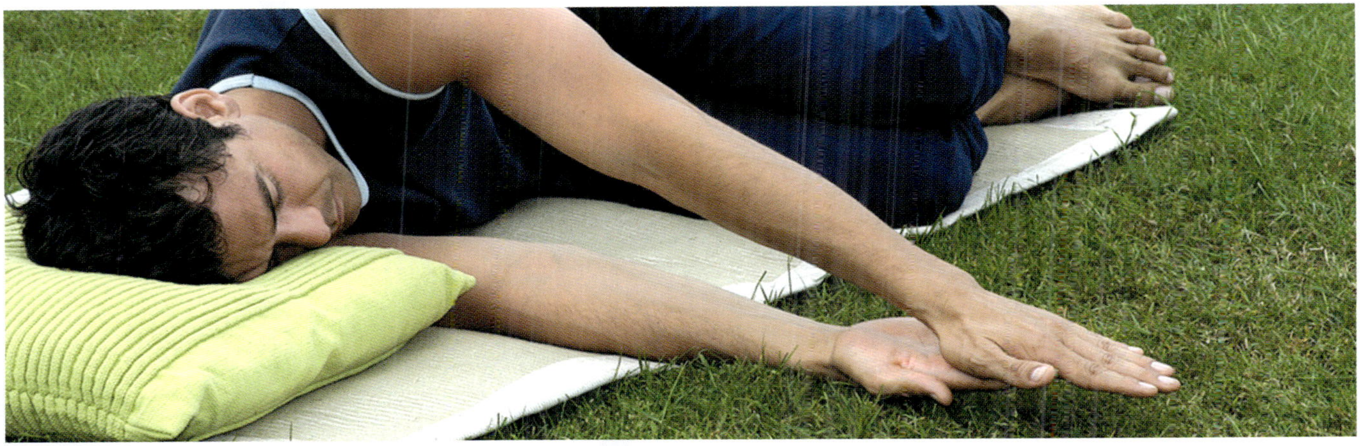

Shoulder Mobility – Relaxation Exercises

Exercise 2: Shoulder Mobility 2

Starting Position

Assume the same position as for Exercise 1 on page 75.

Movement

1. Breathe in to prepare.
2. As you breathe out, keeping the hips and back still, gently stretch the top hand away from the body and lift it towards the sky (A).
3. As you breathe in, return the hand to the starting position.
4. Complete the exercise five times but do not turn over to work the other side until you have completed Exercises 3 and 4.

A.

Shoulder Mobility – Relaxation Exercises

Exercise 3: Shoulder Mobility 3

Starting Position

Assume the same starting position as for Exercise 1 on page 75.

Movement

1. Breathe in to prepare.
2. As you breathe out, stretch the top hand beyond your lower hand.
3. Lift the outstretched hand to the sky and then take it behind your back. Follow this with your eyes so that you turn your head (A).
4. Breathe in as you return to the starting position.
5. Complete the exercise five times but do not turn over until you have completed Exercise 4.

A.

Exercise 4: Shoulder Mobility 4

Starting Position

Assume the same starting position as for Exercise 1 on page 75.

Movement

1. Breathe in to prepare.
2. As you breathe out, keeping the hips and back still, gently stretch the top hand away from the body (A).
3. Lift the outstretched hand to the sky and then take it behind your back. Turn your head as far as possible to follow this movement (B).
4. Now bring the arm over and around the head in an arc (C).
5. Continue the circle and follow the top hand with your eyes until it is reunited with the opposite hand.
6. Turn over and repeat the last four exercises on the other side.

A.

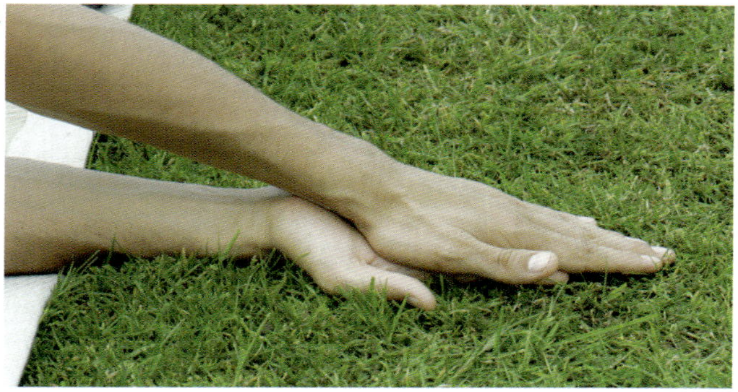

B.

C.

Exercise 5: Shoulder Stretch

A.

Starting Position

Assume the same starting position as for Exercise 1 on page 75.

Movement

1. Breathe in to prepare.
2. As you breathe out, stretch your top hand beyond your lower hand. Lift the top arm in front of the body, then take the hand towards the thigh (A)
3. As you breathe in, stretch the arm back behind the body (B).
4. As you breathe out, return to the starting position.
5. Complete the exercise five times, and then turn over and repeat on the other side.

B.

Exercise 6: Trapezius Stretch

Starting Position

A.

Stand with your feet hip width apart and with your arms in front of you (A).

Movement

1. Link your fingers together and turn the palms out. Keep the elbows relaxed.
2. Take a deep breath and as you do so stretch the shoulders so that the back is extended (B).
3. Hold the position for thirty seconds before returning to the starting position.

B.

Exercise 7: Scapula Stretch

A.

Starting Position

Stand with feet hip width apart with your arms by your sides.

Movement

1. Stretch the right arm out across the front of the body.
2. Keeping the right arm across the body, take hold of it with your left hand and pull it towards you (A).
3. Hold the position for thirty seconds, before returning to the starting position.
4. Reverse the arms and repeat the movement.

Hamstrings and Glutes Exercises

The hamstrings are made up of three muscles situated behind the thigh: biceps femoris (long and short head), semitendinosus and semimembransus. The functions of these muscles are to bend the knee joint, internal and external rotation and hip extension.

The glutials comprises of the gluteus maximus, medius and minimus, which are situated behind the leg at the top of the thigh. These muscles extend and rotate the hip. The gluteus maximus extends and rotates the hip outwards while the gluteus medius flexes and inwardly rotates the hip.

The object of these movements is to stretch the muscles and take out any tension that might have developed during earlier exercises. Each stretch should be held for thirty seconds to help increase flexibility. Keep the back neutral throughout this routine.

Hamstrings and Glutes Exercises

Exercise 1: Hamstring Stretch

Starting Position

Lie on the floor on your back. Bend your knees, placing your feet hip width apart. Relax your shoulders and draw your shoulder blades down towards your waist, pulling them slightly into the centre. Tuck your chin in so the neck feels long. The lumbar spine should be in the neutral position, the hips relaxed and the weight evenly distributed across the buttocks. A resistance band is particularly useful for this exercise (A).

Movement

1. Breathe in to prepare.
2. As you breathe out, draw the right leg up and towards the body. Grab hold of the back of the thigh and pull it further towards the body (B).
3. Hold the position with a flexed foot (C)
4. Breathe in and out for thirty seconds, gradually increasing the stretch.
5. Return to the starting position and repeat with the left leg.

A.

B.

C.

Hamstrings and Glutes Exercises

Exercise 2: Cross Leg Stretch 1

Starting Position

Assume the same starting position as for Exercise 1 on page 83 (A).

Movement

1. Breathe in to prepare.
2. Take your right foot and place it on the knee of your left leg.
3. Place your right hand on the right knee and gently push the knee away (B).
4. Breathe out and, still pushing the knee away, lift the left leg towards the body. Complete five times with each leg.

A.

B.

Exercise 3: Cross Leg Stretch 2

Starting Position

Assume the same starting position as for Exercise 1 on page 83.

Movement

1. Breathe in to prepare.

2. Cross your right leg over the left leg. Hold your left knee with both hands. Breathe out and draw the knees toward the chest (A).

3. Hold the position for thirty seconds and then return to the starting position. Repeat the exercise with the leg positioning reversed.

A.

Hamstrings and Glutes Exercises

Exercise 4: Cross Leg Stretch 3

Starting Position

Assume the same starting position as for Exercise 1 on page 83.

Movement

1. Breathe in to prepare.
2. Cross your right leg over your left leg. Hold your left ankle with your right hand and your right ankle with your left hand. Raise your knees towards your body
3. Breathe out and stretch the legs, pulling them slightly apart (A).
4. Hold the position for thirty seconds. Return to the starting position. Cross the left leg over the right and repeat the stretch.

A.

Hamstrings and Glutes Exercises

Exercise 5: Glutes Stretch

Starting Position

Assume the same starting position as for Exercise 1 on page 83.

Movement

1. Breathe in to prepare.

2. Stretch the right leg towards the sky, flexing the foot (A).

3. Hold the right thigh with your left hand and draw the leg towards your left ear (B).

4. Keeping your back on the floor, hold the position for thirty seconds and then draw the right leg a little nearer the body (C).

5. Return to the starting position and repeat with the other leg.

A.

B.

C.

Hamstrings and Glutes Exercises

Exercise 6: Piriformis Stretch

Starting Position

Lie on the floor with both legs stretched out. Keep the back in contact with the floor throughout the exercise (A).

A.

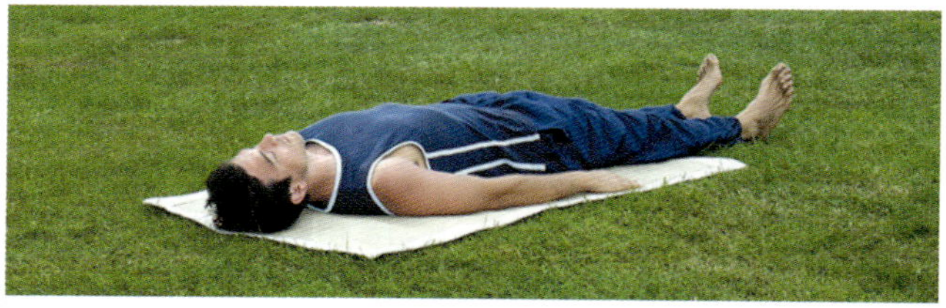

Movement

1. Breathe in and bend the left knee towards the body, so that the thigh is at a right angle to the hip.

2. Take hold of the left knee with the right hand and draw it across the opposite leg, remembering not to lift your back off the floor.

3. You should be able to feel a stretch through the buttock muscles. Hold for a count of thirty.

4. Gently breathe in and return to the starting position. Repeat the stretch with the right leg.

B.

Hamstrings and Glutes Exercises

Exercise 7: Forward Step

Starting Position

Stand with feet hip width apart and your hands by your sides (A).

A.

Movement

1. Take a step forwards on your right foot.
2. Bend your left knee and stretch your right leg from the hip. Place your hands on your left leg.
3. Hold the position, breathing in and out for thirty seconds.
4. Repeat the exercise on your left leg.

B.

Inner Thigh and Other Leg Exercises

The adductor muscles within the inner thigh are: the adductor brevis, the adductor longus and the adductor magnus. They originate in the pubis and ischium and insert into the femur.

The exercises here open the hips out, allowing the inner thighs to relax. Each stretch should be held for thirty seconds to help increase flexibility. Keep the back supported throughout the stretches.

Inner Thigh and Other Leg Exercises

Exercise 1: Adductor Stretch 1

Starting Position

Lie on the floor with your knees bent and your feet together. Keep your shoulders soft and tuck your chin in so that your neck feels long (A).

Movement

1. Breathe in to prepare.

2. As you breathe out, allow the knees to drop to the sides but keep the soles of the feet together (B).

3. Hold for five breaths and then return to the starting position.

4. Complete the exercise five times.

A.

B.

Inner Thigh and Other Leg Exercises

Exercise 2: Adductor Stretch 2

Starting Position

Lie on the floor and stretch your legs up a wall. Rest your buttocks as close to the wall as possible (A).

Movement

1. Breathe in to prepare.

2. As you breathe out, stretch your legs out to the sides (B).

A.

3. Hold this position, gently breathing in and out, for ten breaths.

4. Return to the starting position and complete the exercise five times.

B.

Exercise 3: Gastrocnemius Stretch

Starting Position

Stand in front of a wall with your feet hip width apart. Place your hands on the wall shoulder width apart – your fingers should be pointing upwards, elbows slightly bent. Tuck your chin in so that your neck feels long.

A.

Movement

1. Take a gentle inward breath and step back with the right leg, keeping the heel down.

2. As you breathe out, bend the left knee. You should be able to feel a stretch through the right calf (B).

3. Hold for thirty seconds and repeat the exercise, reversing the leg positions.

B.

Exercise 4: Soleus Stretch

Starting Position

Assume the same starting position as for Exercise 3 on page 93.

Movement

1. Place the toes of the right foot next to the heel of the left foot.
2. Bend both knees, keeping the heels on the floor.
3. Stretch the back of the calves (A).
4. Repeat the exercise, reversing the feet position.

A.

Exercise 5: Quads Stretch

Starting Position

Lie on the floor on your front with your forehead resting on your hands. Keep the shoulders and back relaxed and the neck long (A).

Movement

1. Bend your left leg up.
2. Hold your left foot with your right hand and lift the left thigh off the floor.
3. Hold the position for thirty seconds, gently breathing in and out.
4. Return to the starting position and repeat the exercise on the opposite leg.

A.

B.

Glossary

Abduction: A muscle contraction that draws away from the midline of the body.

Adduction: A muscle contraction that draws inward to the midline of the body.

Cervical vertebrae: The top seven bones in the spinal column which support the neck and head.

Clavicle: The collarbone.

Coccyx: The tailbone.

Disc: Shock-absorbing cartilage between two vertebrae.

Extension: Straightening the limb with muscles.

Flexion: Bending the joint or limb with muscles.

Hyperextension: Straightening out the limb beyond its normal range of motion.

Keeping a neutral spine: Keeping the natural curve in your spine during exercise rather than flattening it out or pressing it into the floor.

Ligament: A band of fibrous tissue that connects bones or cartilage at a joint or supports an organ.

Lumbar: The five large vertebrae in the lower back.

Pelvic girdle: The buttocks and lower back.

Pelvis: The lower part of the abdomen located between the hip bones; the basin-shaped structure that supports the spinal column.

Quadriceps: The large extensor muscle at the front of the thigh.

Rectus abdominal: A section of muscles running down the stomach.

Rotation: Twisting around a central axis.

Sacrum: The five vertebrae above the coccyx and at the top of the pelvis: usually fused together into a triangular bone.

Scapulae: Shoulder blades.

Transverse abdominal: The deepest layer of abdominal muscles which help to stabilise the body's core.

Tricep: The muscle at the back of the upper arm that extends or straightens the elbow.

Vertebrae: The bone segments that form the spinal column.